GROWING BY KNOWING

Growing Your Business by Knowing Your Numbers

By Philippe Lerner; CFO, MBA

& Michael Hammelburger

GROWING BY KNOWING

Growing Your
Business By Knowing
Your Numbers

TABLE *of* CONTENTS

FOREWORD

By Jeff Spokes

Phillippe and Michael have been my bookkeepers for almost 10 years and are my go-to experts when it comes to bookkeeping. In this book they've created a guidepost to understanding your business' finances from the ground up. It's an essential tool if you are building a business and want to do your own accounting OR you'll be hiring an accountant and want to hold them to a higher standard.

As a business owner and customer of PLC Financial for many years, I've asked lots of questions and Phillippe and Michael have been a wealth of knowledge, answering those and guiding me to making good financial decisions.

Take time to read this book, preferably BEFORE you start a business. It describes the types of entity options for your business, some options for bookkeeping software and most importantly how to keep track of your books. I highly encourage you to try the manual mode first when you start out with limited numbers of transactions. Why? It will help you to really understand your business.

Then, when you've created reports and gone through several months of hand-generating those guideposts, move on to financial software. The reports they generate can be eye-opening, illuminating, pointing you directly to cost savings and profit-generating areas of your business. Good luck and profitability!

Jeff Spokes, Spokes Marketing
www.SpokesMarketing.com

INTRODUCTION

How many times have we heard we should be working on our area of expertise inside our business, or our 'highest and best use?' There is great truth to that and not everyone can be good at wearing *every* hat within a small business. Everyone has their area of strength and sometimes it isn't always in the area of financials.

Within a business, there are few things that are more essential yet more overlooked than managing the books. Knowing your numbers is something that every successful business owner does. It doesn't mean that they do all the finances themselves –it means that their books are up to date and they know how their company is doing. Does knowing your numbers guarantee that you'll succeed? Of course not! Knowing your numbers is more like having a GPS on your business. It can direct you on where to go- but you still need to drive the car.

I've found that a business runs best when every person has their area of concentration and can execute it well—a well-oiled machine where all the working parts operate smoothly and in tandem. That is why I advocate for business owners to hire a great CFO; either within or outsource one. That's where we excel!

So many people who own businesses tell us how much they 'hate numbers' and they don't know where to start to learn how to better manage their finance. That's how this book came into existence. After years of teaching and consulting, we wanted to be able to expand our reach and help as many people as we could have a resource where they can simply either read cover to cover or just open up the sections they need brushing up on.

Wouldn't it be great if the burden of doing your year-end bookwork was lifted from your shoulders? Or what about straightening out your bank statements? Or managing your accounts receivables? Just imagine if someone could help you make future projections and plan accordingly! The first step is acknowledging that your business could use an extra expert to help create a more profitable bottom line, allowing your business to grow while you are free to pursue the areas of *your strength* in your company.

We sincerely hope that you find value in our book and we encourage your comments and overall feedback. We're here to help inform and educate you on the world of accounting so you can make better decisions.

We wish you happy reading and a prosperous business;

Philippe & Michael

Chapter One

WHY DO I NEED
A BOOKKEEPING SYSTEM?

Business owners who have tried unsuccessfully to tackle the whole 'bookkeeping thing' end up asking this question out of frustration. If you can relate to this sentiment in any way, I want you to know you have my empathy; you really do. The

17

point is, that if you are establishing in a business, you need a bookkeeping system. Some business's bookkeeping systems consist solely of a shoebox stuffed full of receipts. This is one way to do it, but not the most effective way. For one thing, this way will cost you a lot when you hand your shoebox to your 'very-expensive-per-hour-accountant' at tax time who will charge you to sort it all out for you when you could have done it yourself throughout the year. A good bookkeeping system is easy to maintain daily, weekly, or monthly, depending on your volume of transactions.

Use your bookkeeping system to keep track of your cash flow: your money coming in and your money going out. You can break down your expenses so you can see how much is going to what areas of your business each month. Likewise, you can break down your income so you can see what areas are most profitable. Keep track of your equipment and major purchases you have made to run your business. A bookkeeping system will allow you to stay on top of your bank accounts and investments and keep track of your draws plus provide you with a system to bill your customers while keeping track of account receivables. Very handy!

Also, create a system for paying bills and keeping track of accounts payable (who you owe) so you can make payments on time and save yourself that extra finance charge. That way you won't end up paying for things twice. Do your own taxes, payroll, state and otherwise. The list is endless however, so are the good reasons for having a well-maintained bookkeeping system. You really <u>can</u> do all these things!

This may sound like a long list of things to do but if you do it periodically, in small amounts, instead of once a year, it is easy and manageable. The rest of this book will break down all the 'how's and why's' of getting yourself up and running in an easy-to-manage bookkeeping system of your own. If you are using an easy accounting software program on your computer, this book will help you understand why things are entered in a certain way.

If you are going to be keeping your bookkeeping system manually, let me suggest you get a few columnar books. Get a couple which have 3 columns (one you can mark 'plus,' one for 'minus' and one for 'balance'). On each page, you can set up one of your general ledger accounts and keep track of each transaction you make. As you read the following chapters you will see how this will be helpful, and you can set it all up in one big notebook.

Or, have a couple of notebooks— one as a "sales" or 'income journal," one as an "expense journal." You can keep it as simple as you want. These activities will help you keep up the habit of entering your transactions that I am about to describe on the upcoming pages. You may also want to get one of the larger 13 column books so you can create a spreadsheet on various sections, such as your total income or expenses, compare them with the months before, and so forth. As you read on I hope to help you develop some good methods and practices. Just remember keep it simple!

Part One: Set Up Your 'Chart of Accounts' and Filing System

What is a 'Chart of Accounts?' This is your list of General Ledger Accounts which is the map of everything financial in your company. In your Chart of Accounts you have several sections. I will briefly explain them as we go along. Later I will explain how they fit together, how you make entries to them, and why you need them set up this way. So here they are, in order:

1) **Assets:** This is where you set up everything and anything which will be an asset to your company for a period of time (months or years). "Current" Assets are accounts such as Bank accounts, your Accounts receivables (those are the accounts of your customers who owe you money on time, not cash sales), or Inventory, to name a few. "Fixed" assets are, for example, the value of major equipment purchases, ("Fixed" means they aren't going anywhere unless you get rid of them), and the "fair market value" of land or property owned by your business, or anything that continually adds to the worth of your company.

2) **Liabilities:** These are the debts your company accumulates to be paid at a later date, or to be continually paid on for long periods of time. If there is a loan to your company, the rule of thumb for judging a "Long Term" Liability versus a

"Current" Liability is this: if the loan period is a year or longer, it is a Long Term Liability. Anything owed which will take less than a year to pay off is a Current Liability. Some examples of Liability Accounts are: Loans made to your company (car loans, equipment loans, property loans), Accounts Payable (those are the accounts of your vendors that you owe money to 'on time,' not cash purchases), any Taxes Payable accounts (payroll taxes, your state's sales tax, or federal taxes that are accumulated as you conduct business and are paid periodically).

3) **Equity:** This is where you keep track of what you personally put into and take out of the company. These are your Draw Accounts (money you remove from the company for personal use), Owner Investment Account (money you have taken from your personal resources and injected into your business). This is also an area where you can list your company's Retained Earnings and Net Income Accounts. Your Net Income shows your company's Net Profits for a given time period and is accumulated throughout your company's fiscal year. This account will start over again from zero with the

new fiscal year. The Retained Earnings Account is where your cumulative Net Profit is reflected, ("Retained"), on a permanent basis. This account does not zero-out at any time. It continues to reflect the fiscal year changes in your Net Profits from year to year.

4) **Income**: Just as it describes, these are the sales received from your customers whether you have sent them a bill or made a cash sale. This is the category under which it is recorded. (More on how that works later on.) This is also a place to list Reimbursed Expenses, which act as an offsetting account to certain expenses, such as shipping or travel expenses.

5) **Cost of Goods Sold**: These are your first Expense Accounts where you record purchases made for the sole purpose of operating your business. Things like 'Merchandise for Inventory,' if you're in retail, or parts that go into the machines you make, or food, beer and wine for your restaurant, or gravel and asphalt for the roads you pave. You get the idea. Some people also like to

include in this section Wages Paid, or Shipping Costs.

6) **General and Administrative Expenses**: These are your next set of Expense Accounts. These accounts come under the sub-headings of things like Bank Charges, Consultation Fees, Donations, Equipment Rental, Finance Charges, Maintenance and Repair, Utilities, Entertainment and Travel, Licenses, Permits, Professional Services (lawyers and accountants), Wages, and any expensed taxes like Payroll, State or Federal Taxes, Auto Expenses, Insurance, and on and on. If you are just starting out and you want to keep it simple, here is a good rule of thumb: get a free copy of the Schedule C for tax form 1040 from the IRS:
http://www.irs.ustreas.gov/formspubs/index.html.

Use this as a guideline for setting up your General Expense accounts. It has every expense that the IRS allows for a small business (in particular a sole proprietorship), to report at tax time. These are the ones that count. You may find that you want to make your expense accounts more detailed so they make more sense to your particular situation. You can do this as the need arises and you can break down your expense accounts at any time as you go along, but the Schedule C is a good starting guide.

7) Other Income and Expenses: Finally—last section! This has two areas in one. 'Other Income' is Interest Income, or Uncategorized or Miscellaneous Income accounts. The nebulous stuff can be held here until you find a better place for it. It actually is better if you can stay away from using the Uncategorized or Miscellaneous accounts if possible as it will be one less explanation you have to make should anyone of importance come to scrutinize your "details." That's why I say, just use it until you find a better place to put it. I check my Miscellaneous Accounts once a month. They are like little flags that let me know there is something I need to deal with before I close off the month's business. Other Expenses are a little different from Other Income. Other Expenses is where to put things like Depreciation Expense and Amortization Expense (I will explain how you incur these expenses later on.) Generally, these are expense accounts that don't have a direct effect on the running of your business, but are still a part of your monthly financial picture. There are also

Uncategorized or Miscellaneous Expense accounts, just like the Other Income accounts, and the same suggestion for use of these accounts applies in this area as well.

On the next page there is an example of a Chart of Accounts for a typical retail business as a Sole Proprietorship.

Note: These following examples are based on the Sole Proprietorship style of business setup, as it is the easiest as far as filing taxes at the end of the year and a good way to start out if you are new and want a simple setup. However, based on your unique specifications, such as how large your company will be, your volume of expected income, or how many people involved in running it, you may want to consider other setups such as an S-Corporation or an LLC, for example. You should thoroughly explore the tax and legal benefits of other types of business setups. If you are interested in other forms of businesses you should definitely consult the advice of your CPA or lawyer. Also, please note however, that for our purposes in this book, the basic bookkeeping setup explained on the following pages is the same no matter what style of business you choose to set up. The only difference is corporations and LLCs may have a few additional general ledger accounts not mentioned here. But bookkeeping and accounting basics are all the same for any business!

Chart of Accounts

Business Checking: Asset

Business Savings: Asset

Accounts Receivable: Asset

Inventory: Asset

Major Equipment: Asset (Fixed)

Equipment Depreciation: Asset (Fixed)

Accounts Payable: Liability (Current)

Payroll Tax Payable: Liability (Current)

State Sales Tax Payable: Liability (Current)

Federal Tax Payable: Liability (Current)

Bank Note Payable: Liability (Long Term or Current)

Auto Loan Payable: Liability (Long Term or Current)

Owner Draws: Equity

Owner Investment: Equity

Net Income: Equity

Retained Earnings: Equity

Resale Income: Income

Wholesale Income: Income

Discounts and Returns: Income

Reimbursed Expenses: Income

Resale Merchandise: Cost of Goods Sold

Advertising: Expense

Automobile Expenses: Expense

Bank Charges: Expense

Contributions: Expense

Dues and Subscriptions: Expense

Equipment Rental: Expense

Insurance: Expense

Interest Expense: Expense

Licenses and Permits: Expense

Payroll Wages: Expense

Payroll Taxes: Expense

Postage and Delivery: Expense

Professional Fees: Expense

Rent: Expense

Repairs and Maintenance: Expense

Supplies: Expense

Taxes-State & Federal: Expense

Travel and Entertainment: Expense

Utilities: Expense

Interest Income: Other Income

Miscellaneous Income: Other Income

Depreciation Expense: Other Expense

Miscellaneous Expense: Other Expense

This is just a basic start-up listing of a Chart of Accounts. As you record financial entries for your business, each of these accounts will provide homes for all of those entries. As I mentioned earlier, when you get farther along in your business, you may find a need for more detailed accounts or even 'Sub-Accounts' (e.g. Auto Expense can have Sub-Accounts for Fuel and Repairs, or Utilities can have Sub-Accounts of Telephone and Electricity), so that your list of General Ledger Accounts makes more sense to you.

Once you figure out what accounts you want to start your Chart of Accounts with, you will want to create a file system to maintain all the paperwork, i.e. receipts, bank statements, all utility bills, any tax forms (such as payroll or sales tax), and invoices from purchases you have made for your business. For a simple start-up filing system, I find it easiest to just get a box of large manila envelopes. I keep the receipts, bank statements, invoices and tax forms for each month in one of the envelopes. I mark the outside of the envelope "JULY 2008," for example, and then just simply put all the paper for that month into that envelope and put it in a storage box that contains all of 2008.

Or, if you know your business is going to be larger and a little more complicated than that, get a file cabinet. Keep your paper in alphabetical order in file folders in the file drawers and then clean it out into a well-marked box once a year. Once you get a handle on your filing system, here are some parameters on how long you must keep all the important papers you will be accumulating:

Keep for 3 Years:
Bank statements
Deposit slips
Insurance policies
General correspondence

Keep for 4 years:
Invoices to customers
Cash expenditure receipts
Expense reports by/for employees

Keep for 7 years:
Accounts payable documents
Accounts receivable documents
Cancelled checks
Notes receivable paperwork (paid off)
Payroll records
Employee/personnel records
Inventory records and invoices

Keep Permanently:

Chart of accounts/General ledgers

Legal correspondence

Mortgage paperwork

Financial statements

Notes payable paperwork

Property appraisals and records

Tax returns and related documents

Trademark registrations

I know what you are thinking! Yes, it does pile up! And, fast too! I know some small businesses that are so big and old they have to actually *rent* a storage space just to keep all their old paperwork in. But make no mistake here; it is well worth it! If you ever get audited for anything by any government agency, there is absolutely no greater satisfaction than to be able to quickly and easily put your hands on the pile of paper they want to examine!

Or, think of this situation: What if you have to prove you've paid for something and when you paid it? Or, what if you have to prove to someone they never paid you when you billed them? So, make certain you create a good filing system from the beginning and keep all the old paperwork for the recommended amount of time. Eventually you will be very glad you did!

Entering Your Information
(The Core of Accounting Principles)

What I am about to explain here is really the core of accounting principles. Once you get this mode of thinking down, you will have everything you need to master these principles. Seriously, clear your mind right now of the way your bank talks to you, and of balance sheets or any other financial statements. Just focus on this and very soon you will see how it all fits together.

In bookkeeping you always make entries called "Double Sided Entries." That means for every one entry made there has to be a counter entry made. These are called Debits and Credits. Regarding your General Ledger Accounts, a Debit can be a plus OR a minus, and a Credit can be a plus OR a minus. This all depends on what account you are dealing with. Are you with me so far? Okay, that's one thing to remember.

Depending on how an amount gets ADDED to an account determines if that account is called a

Debit Account or a Credit Account. So, remember the Chart of Accounts from the previous pages? This is how these accounts are classified according to Debits and Credits:

Asset = Debit
Liability = Credit
Equity = Credit
Income = Credit
Cost of Goods Sold = Debit
Expense = Debit
Other Income = Credit
Other Expense = Debit

When REMOVING amounts from your general ledger accounts, the amount removed is the opposite from the debit or credit, whichever is appropriate. (Examples are coming up!) Our list of general ledger accounts for the sake of double-sided entries will function this way:

Asset Accounts: Debit = (+) Credit = (-)
Liability Accounts: Debit = (-) Credit = (+)
Equity Accounts: Debit = (-) Credit = (+)
Income Accounts: Debit = (-) Credit = (+)

Cost of Goods Sold: Debit = (+) Credit = (-)

Expense Accounts: Debit = (+) Credit = (-)

Other Income Accounts: Debit = (-) Credit = (+)

Other Expense Accounts: Debit = (+) Credit = (-)

When you make your entries, remember, all your entries have to have *counter entries*. This is how we keep the "books in balance." An easy way to start out on this new way of thinking is to imagine a "T." As you are figuring out what goes where, it helps to take a piece of paper and draw this T. On the LEFT side of the T write "Debit" (can be abbreviated DR, don't ask me why), and on the RIGHT side of the T write "Credit" (can be abbreviated using CR), like this: DR I CR. These are called "T Accounts." Appropriate! (Note: Debit is always on the left and Credit is always on the right regardless if either is a plus or a minus.) Okay, I know you are dying to see this in action, so let's do a simple entry using the "T Accounts." Say you need some paper and an ink cartridge for your printer, and you also noticed your supply of pens have somehow all walked out the door. You go to your neighborhood office supply store with your company check book, write out a check for these items, and take them back to your office. Now you need to log your purchase. If you have a neat accounting program on your computer, you just call up your check register, enter the date, check number, who the check was written to, the amount, designate "Office Supplies" for your account, and in "Memo" write "Pens, Paper and Ink," hit enter and you're done! But what your accounting software is actually doing for you is based on our "T Accounts." The entry the software made looks like this:

Checking
DR I CR
$25.00

Office Supplies
DR I CR
$25.00

So what actually took place was this: Cash was REMOVED from the Checking Account, which is an Asset Account, which means it is a Debit Account, so when we remove an amount from that account it is a CREDIT entry. The other thing that took place was we ADDED to the Office Supplies, which is an Expense Account, which means it also is a Debit Account, so when we add to that account, it is a DEBIT entry. See how the T Accounts can give you a physical picture of what is *actually* going to where? No? Let's do another simple entry; say someone comes into your place and wants to purchase some merchandise. They are going to pay for it on the spot so it is a cash sale. You are a retailer, therefore, if you are in most states, you must also charge sales tax, which you accumulate and pay all at once to the state at a later time. Here's how this entry looks in:

T Accounts:
Checking
DR I CR
$52.50

Sales
DR I CR
$50.00

Sales Tax Payable
DR I CR
$2.50

See how we used two credit entries to balance the one debit entry? This is why we ADDED to the Checking Account, which is an Asset Account and therefore a Debit Account, so when we add to that account it is a DEBIT entry. We also ADDED to the Sales Account, which is an Income Account and therefore a Credit Account. So when we add to that account, it is a CREDT entry. Lastly, we also ADDED to the Sales Tax Payable Account, which is a Liability Account (because we are accumulating it to be paid at a later date) so when we add to that account it is also a CREDIT entry. By the way, if you live in a state with Sales Tax a helpful resource is your state's tax agency's website. In Washington it is http://dor.wa.gov.

I'll show you a couple more appropriate entries. Say you have a really good regular customer. They buy retail (as opposed to wholesale) so you have to charge sales tax, as most states require it. They call up and want you to send them some merchandise in the mail and they will pay you thirty days later, so they want to be billed them for the product. This one transaction would have two series of entries to follow through with. Here's how it looks in T Accounts:

Entry #1:

Retail Sales

DR I CR

$50.00

Sales Tax Payable

DR I CR

$2.50

Shipping (Reimbursed Expense)

DR I CR

$2.50

Accounts Receivable ("Mr. Really Good Customer")

DR I CR

$55.00

The balance of Mr. Really Good Customer's account is now being stored in your Accounts Receivable Account. Which is an Asset account, therefore a Debit account and we ADDED to it so this one Debit entry was balanced out using three

Credit entries. Did you follow along? Here is the flip side to this:

Entry #2: (Mr. Really Good Customer pays 30 days later):

Checking
DR I CR
$55.00

Accounts Receivable
DR I CR
$55.00

Now that the customer paid, you will ADD his payment to the Checking Account and REMOVE the balance that he owes you from your Accounts Receivable account. Do you see the "ins" and "outs" of this and why it is logged this way? It's important to record a transaction on the day the transaction was completed. Recording transactions another time is the cause of many headaches and a great deal of puzzlement in bookkeeping! Let's say that when Mr. Really Good Customer called on September 20th. Maybe it took you two days to get everything together for his order and you shipped it on September 23rd. Now September 23rd is the date on his invoice that you sent to him with his order, but Mr. Really Good Customer won't be sending you a check until October 20th. Even though your checking account will not reflect his payment until October, you still need to show that the sale was made in September. This is for the sake of budgeting, forecasting, and comparison. That is why there is an Accounts Receivable account to store customer balances until they pay and that is why there needs to be two series of entries for this one transaction.

Note: This is called "Accrual Based" accounting, (as opposed to "Cash Based" accounting). In Cash Based accounting there is no need for this because everything is recorded as sold, or paid, as the transaction takes place. You only record the transaction as you write the check for the expense, or receive the money for the bill owed to you. Because of this, Cash Based accounting is a little easier. In the Cash Based accounting method, debits and credits and all the principles we have discussed so far still apply. But, I personally like Accrual Based accounting as a more effective way of avoiding problems in cash flow, budgeting and so forth. This is because we are recording the transactions on the date they occur and storing them in our assets or liabilities until they are to be paid or received, this way we can plan ahead and make well-educated business decisions, and manage cash flow better. So in these past explanations, and those to follow, keep in mind I am basing my methods on Accrual Based accounting. Of course, you may choose to set up your small business based on either method. You should make a decision on one method or the other to keep your bookkeeping system consistent. Also, when tax time comes around you should tell your accountant under which system you are operating; Accrual or Cash Based. Once you start filing a certain way with your state government or the IRS, you shouldn't change it from year to year.

It works exactly the same way with your Accounts Payable Account. Think in reverse. You receive a bill for some merchandise you ordered, and you are the Really Good Customer, but you are buying wholesale because you are intending to resell it to your customer, at which point you will add on sales tax. (If you are in a state where sales tax is charged, you will not be paying tax on this merchandise at your point of purchase, but your customer will pay sales tax when he buys it from you.) You have thirty days to pay, and for all the same reasons, you want to record that expense according to the date on the invoice that your vendor sent to you. Your transaction for this is also two series of entries. It looks like this:

Entry #1:

Resale Merchandise (Cost of Goods Sold)
DR I CR
$50.00

Shipping (Expense Account)
DR I CR
$2.50

Accounts Payable (Acme Merchandise)
DR I CR
$52.50

Your Accounts Payable account is a Liability, therefore a Credit account. Now, when we ADD to Accounts Payable it is a Credit entry. Do you see how it took the two Debit entries to balance the one Credit entry? Now you are holding your balance due to Acme Merchandise in your Accounts Payable account until you get ready to pay it thirty days later. You want to record your expense in the month in which it was incurred. So, now it's thirty days later, you're paying your bills, and here is the flip side to this transaction:

Entry #2:

Checking
DR I CR
$52.50

Accounts Payable
DR I CR
$52.50

Are you seeing how this is working together? Okay, one more transaction and this one is a bit complex. If you can follow along on this one, you don't need to read this chapter over again! Say you want to buy a machine for your shop. It will cost $10,000.00! You don't happen to have the cash available so you go to the bank. They say okay and give you five years to pay it off at 5% interest. (Nice Bank!) This will take one major transaction and five years-worth of monthly transactions to accomplish. However, once you set it up, it will be no problem. Here's how this looks in T Accounts:

Main Entry:

Capitalized Equipment
DR I CR
$10,000.00

Note Payable (Nice Bank)
DR I CR
$10,000.00

Well, that part was easy. The Capitalized Equipment is a Fixed Asset Account. This is where you will hold the full value of your equipment, to be depreciated monthly over the next five years. (We will discuss Depreciation in greater detail later on.) This is good because beefing up your assets makes your company look pretty good on paper to the people who care about things like that. The Note Payable to the Nice Bank is now a Long Term Liability Account, because it will take you five years to pay it off. So, here are the entries you will be making on a monthly basis to reduce the note, record the interest expense and depreciate the equipment:

#1: Note Reduction:
Checking
DR ǀ CR
$189.00

Note Payable-Nice Bank
DR ǀ CR
$147.00

Interest Expense
DR ǀ CR
$42.00
#2: Depreciation Expense:

Accumulated Depreciation

DR I CR

$167.00

Depreciation Expense

DR I CR

$167.00

OK, what did we do?? Well, the time came to make your first payment. Using your handy loan calculation program on your computer, OR getting the loan payment amortization schedule from your Nice Bank, you saw your monthly payment was to be $189.00 per month. Out of this, a portion goes to the principle on the note and the rest is interest expense. Take advantage of interest expense as a write off against profits, while the principle portion of your payment reduces your Liabilities by reducing your Note Payable. The loan payment amortization schedule is a handy thing to have because it shows exactly what the portions are each month so you can keep in step with the bank. If you don't have one for your loans, get one! Next, you might want to call your CPA to find out about depreciation. You can do this yourself on a monthly basis. The rule of thumb is to take the value of the equipment and divide it, for example, by 60 months, which is 5 years. This is the "Straight Line Depreciation Method" and is based on the assumption that the average life of your asset is five years. Time periods may vary depending on the type of asset it is —land, computers, heavy equipment, signage, etc. If you are unsure, this is a question worthy of your CPA's time. Otherwise, it is a very simple way to capture your depreciation expense on a monthly basis. Your CPA may make an adjustment to this at the end of the year. The Accumulated Depreciation Account is a "Negative Asset" account. It immediately follows the Capitalized Equipment Account. It is an Asset Account, but you add to it by making a Credit entry, it will appear as having a negative balance on your financial reports. This is correct and as it should be. You are slowly reducing the value of your fixed assets with depreciation. Taking depreciation on your capital assets can save you a lot in taxes. It is a good way to add to your expenses to reduce your profits without affecting your cash flow.

	A	B	C	D	E	F
1	**Sample Chart of Accounts**					
2	Account Name	Code	Financial Statement	Group	Sub-Group	Normally
3	Bank checking account	100	Balance sheet	Current assets	Cash and cash equivalents	Debit
4	Bank savings account	110	Balance sheet	Current assets	Cash and cash equivalents	Debit
5	Online savings account	120	Balance sheet	Current assets	Cash and cash equivalents	Debit
6	Petty cash account	130	Balance sheet	Current assets	Cash and cash equivalents	Debit
7	Paypal account	140	Balance sheet	Current assets	Cash and cash equivalents	Debit
8	Short term marketable securities	200	Balance sheet	Current assets	Short term marketable securities	Debit
9	Accounts receivable	300	Balance sheet	Current assets	Accounts receivable	Debit
10	Allowance for doubtful debts account	310	Balance sheet	Current assets	Accounts receivable	Credit
11	Raw materials	400	Balance sheet	Current assets	Inventory	Debit
12	Work in progress	410	Balance sheet	Current assets	Inventory	Debit
13	Finished goods	420	Balance sheet	Current assets	Inventory	Debit
14	Other receivables	500	Balance sheet	Current assets	Other current assets	Debit
15	Prepayments	510	Balance sheet	Current assets	Other current assets	Debit
16	Long term marketable securities	600	Balance sheet	Long term assets	Long term marketable securities	Debit
17	Property	700	Balance sheet	Long term assets	Property, plant and equipment	Debit
18	Property Depreciation	710	Balance sheet	Long term assets	Property, plant and equipment	Credit
19	Plant	720	Balance sheet	Long term assets	Property, plant and equipment	Debit
20	Plant depreciation	730	Balance sheet	Long term assets	Property, plant and equipment	Credit
21	Equipment	740	Balance sheet	Long term assets	Property, plant and equipment	Debit
22	Equipment depreciation	750	Balance sheet	Long term assets	Property, plant and equipment	Credit
23	Goodwill	800	Balance sheet	Long term assets	Goodwill	Debit
24	Intellectual property	810	Balance sheet	Long term assets	Intellectual property	Debit
25	Intellectual property amortization	820	Balance sheet	Long term assets	Intellectual property	Credit
26	Other assets	840	Balance sheet	Long term assets	Other long term assets	Debit
27	Notes payable	900	Balance sheet	Current liabilities	Notes payable	Credit
28	Accounts payable	1000	Balance sheet	Current liabilities	Accounts payable	Credit

There, was that painless? This is the way things get entered into your General Ledger Accounts, so if you are working late one night and catching up all the transactions of your business day, you will know you did everything 100% correctly IF at the end of all your entries, your Debits EQUAL your Credits. By now, I'm sure you see how this is one of your main goals in entering your information. If you are doing this all manually, without the aid of a nifty, easy to use accounting software program on your computer, you should definitely take the time to add

49

up both sides of your columns. If for some reason your Debits do not equal your Credits, you must find out where you are "out of balance" and make the necessary correction. Because if you don't, you may be chasing a bookkeeping "ghost" for a while and that is a headache! If you are using a handy accounting software program, it probably will not let you record the transaction if you are out of balance in any way.

That's just the way they are, and that is a good thing!

Chapter Two

THE BASIC FINANCIAL
REPORTS

There are many financial reports that you can make for your company based on all your entries collectively. You can get as detailed and as complex as you want. You can make as many reports as you want to suit your needs. You can make reports for budgeting, forecasting or planning. You can make them just on your sales or just on your expenses. If you use a spreadsheet program, you can really go to town!

But, for the sake of simplicity— (our main goal here— I will just discuss the three basic financial reports that are necessary to every business. They are as follows: the Trial Balance, the Profit and Loss (or Income Statement), and the Balance Sheet. You should try to do these monthly or at least quarterly or every 3 months. Don't wait to do them bi-annually or annually. If there are any errors to be corrected, it is much easier to remember back a couple weeks ago than eight months ago! In addition to that, when you see how useful this information is, you will want to utilize it on a regular basis to aid yourself in budgeting, forecasting, and planning.

#1 The Trial Balance

This is, as you may suspect from the name, a 'test' report to make sure all your Debits equal your Credits. The entire Chart of Accounts, that is all your general ledger accounts, are listed. Their current balances, as of whatever day you choose, are listed in either the Debit column or Credit column, depending on if they are Debit Accounts or Credit Accounts. This is just one long list without discernment to whether they are assets, liabilities, expenses, etc. Here is an example of a Trial Balance with a very simple Chart of Accounts, for the months of January thru September:

Trial Balance Jan. 1st - Sept. 30th

Cash in Bank (debit amount) 7,000.00

Accounts Receivable (debit amount) 599.00

Capitalized Equipment (debit amount) 3,200.00

Owner Draws (debit amount) 567.96

Retained Earnings (debit amount) 255.00

Advertising (debit amount) 5.00

Office Supplies (debit amount) 281.94

Postage and Delivery (debit amount) 84.42

Rent (debit amount) 40.00

Taxes (debit amount) 1749.00

Telephone (debit amount) 23.41

Business Meals (debit amount) 166.72

Business Travel (debit amount) 730.05

Depreciation Expense (debit amount) 479.97

Total debit amounts = 15,182.47

Accumulated Depreciation (credit amount) 799.97

Federal Taxes Payable (credit amount) 99.00

Owner Investments (credit amount) 3200.00

Consulting Income (credit amount) 10725.00

Other Regular Income (credit amount) 358.50

Total credit amounts = 15,182.47

See how this goes? This is a great Trial Balance because all the balances in the Debit column add up to the same amount as all the balances in the Credit column. If you try making your Trial Balance and the debits do not equal the credits, guess what? You have to go back and find out where you have made your mistake. If you are doing this manually, it could take some work, however it really is worth the trouble to find the error.

You can start by making certain you have made all your entries through the date you have chosen for your report. For instance, are all your Accounts Receivable Invoices entered? Are all the payments you have received from your customers entered? Have you entered all the checks you have written through this date and are they entered to the correct accounts? Did you enter a Debit amount as a Credit amount (or vice versa)? Have you reconciled your checking account to your bank statement, etc. (This is another great reason to have a simple accounting software program; problems of this nature will be very rare!) So when your Trial Balance is in check, you can move on to the next reports.

A Bookkeeping Trick: take the amount your debits and credits are off by and divide it in two. If it can be divided by two, this is a good indication the problem could be an amount incorrectly entered as a debit or a credit when it should be the other way around. Try this test first, it may make problem solving easier. This same test also applies to balancing your bank accounts to their statements. A check could have been entered incorrectly as a deposit, or vice versa.

#2 The Profit and Loss (or Income) Statement

To make it simple, I just call this report the "P & L." Now is the time to start segregating the General Ledger accounts into their respective classifications. This is a report on the Income, Cost of Goods Sold, Expenses, Other Income and Other Expense accounts apart from the General Ledger Chart of Accounts. Here is an example of a "P & L" using the information from the Trial Balance listed previously:

Profit & Loss Statement Jan. 1st - Sept. 30th

Income
Consulting Income 10,725.00
Other Regular Income 358.50
Total Income 11,083.50

Expenses
Advertising 5.00

Office Supplies 281.94

Postage and Delivery 84.42

Rent 40.00

Taxes (Federal) 1749.00

Telephone 23.41

Meals 166.72

Travel 730.05

Total Expense 3,080.54

Other Expense

Depreciation 479.97

Total Other Expense 479.97

Net Income 7,522.99

Account Title	Unadjusted Trial Balance		Adjustments		Adjusted Trial Balance	
	Debit	Credit	Debit	Credit	Debit	Credit
CASH	10430.00				10430.00	
ACCOUNTS RECEIVABLE	5900.00				5900.00	
SUPPLIES	22807.00			18480.00	4327.00	
PREPAID RENT	24000.00			12000.00	12000.00	
EQUIPMENT	37000.00				37000.00	
ACCU DEPRECIATION				1100.00		1100.00
ACCOUNTS PAYABLE		5200.00				5200.00
NOTES PAYABLE		30537.00				30537.00
UTILITIES PAYABLE		3964.00				3964.00
INTEREST PAYABLE				150.00		150.00
SERVICE REVENUE		82600.00				82600.00
WAGES EXPENSE	18200.00				18200.00	
SUPPLIES EXPENSE			18480.00		18480.00	
RENT EXPENSE			12000.00		12000.00	
DEPRECIATION EXPENSE			1100.00		1100.00	
ELECTRICITY EXPENSE	2470.00				2470.00	
TELEPHONE EXPENSE	1494.00				1494.00	
INTEREST EXPENSE			150.00		150.00	
Totals	122301.00	122301.00	31730.00	31730.00	123551.00	123551.00

Do you see how I got the Net Income figure? This is an important figure because it will be carried onto the next (and final) report, which is the Balance Sheet, coming up. But first, please note this P & L does not have a Cost of Goods Sold section, because it is not a retail or manufacturing company but a service company, therefore it has no Cost of Goods Sold accounts. If you have Cost of Goods Sold accounts to add to your report, they will fit in between the Income and the Expense account sections and will be subtracted from the Income total like the other Expense sections.

Now, all Income, Cost of Goods Sold, and Expense accounts have one thing in common, and that is at the end of the company's fiscal year, all these totals get "zeroed- out." If you are on an easy-to-use accounting software program, this will take place automatically. If you are doing this manually, these entries will have to be made manually. Your Income accounts will all have Debit entries to zero them out. Your cost of goods sold and expense accounts will all have Credit entries to zero them out. Your balancing entry against all these will be to your Retained Earnings account; this is the total of all the entries of both the Debits and Credits. This is explained in more detail in the next report, the "Balance Sheet."

Once again, please note that this report is for the time period Jan. 1st through Sept. 30th and the account totals are the year to date totals for that period. You can do a P & L report any time. You can do it for a day, a week, a month, a year. You can create percentages of your expense accounts against your income. For instance, in the example above, the total expense for Federal Taxes so far through this point in this company's fiscal year is 15.78% (!) of the total income figure. You can also use percentages of expense and income to plan your purchasing better. How much you are making compared to how much you are spending in a certain area or department? You can do comparison P & L's. You can have two columns on your report one with a heading of August Current Year the other with August Previous Year and list the accounts as usual with each of those month's totals. You can use this report for budgeting and forecasting. Make a simulated P & L for next year and see how you do when you make your actual P & L. See the eleven billion uses for this report!

Let's see how it fits together with the next report…

Projected Profit and Loss Statement

	FY2013	FY2014	FY2015
Income	$501,200	$576,380	$662,837
Direct Cost	$177,680	$204,332	$234,981
Gross Margin	$323,520	$372,048	$427,856
Gross Margin %	65%	65%	65%
Expenses			
Salary	$123,900	$135,450	$162,829
Employee Related Expenses	$30,993	$33,864	$40,708
Marketing & Promotion	$24,866	$27,420	$30,521
Rent	$88,000	$88,000	$88,000
Utilities	$3,600	$3,600	$3,600
Leased Equipment	$1,800	$1,800	$1,800
Insurance	$4,200	$4,500	$4,725
Starting Expenses	$13,300	$0	$0
Total Expenses	$290,659	$294,634	$332,183
Operating Income	$32,861	$77,414	$95,673
Interest Incurred	$7,966	$7,354	$5,942
Depreciation and Amortization	$12,320	$12,540	$12,540
Income Taxes	$3,144	$14,380	$19,298
Net Profit	$9,431	$43,140	$57,893
Net Profit/Sales	2%	7%	9%

#3 The Balance Sheet

The Balance Sheet is a report on Assets, Liabilities and Equity. One reason this is called the Balance Sheet is because the total amount of your Assets must equal the sum of your Liabilities + Equity.

Assets = Liabilities + Equity

If that takes place, then you know you have done a good job in putting together your Balance Sheet. Here is an example of a Balance Sheet using the information from the Trial Balance listed previously:

Balance Sheet Jan. 1st - Sept. 30th

Assets

Cash in Bank 7,000.00

Accounts Receivable 599.00

Capitalized Equipment 3,200.00

Accumulated Depreciation -799.97

Total Assets 9,999.03

Liabilities

Federal Tax Payable 99.00

Equity

Owner Investment 3,200.00

Owner Draws -567.96

Retained Earnings -255.00

Net Income 7,522.99

Total Liabilities & Equity 9,999.03

This is a great Balance Sheet because the total of all the Asset balances is the same as when the Liabilities are added to the Equity Accounts.

Now that you have an example in front of you, let's talk a little about the Balance Sheet. This is a report on all your accounts that have continuous balances. The General Ledger accounts reported on here do NOT get "zeroed- out" at the end of the fiscal year and turned over. They are on-going, reflecting the changes accordingly as you add to them, or take from them, for the duration of the company. There are only two exceptions in these accounts. They are the Owner Draw account and Net Income. At the beginning of every fiscal year, the balances in these two accounts are zero. This is true for the draw account because imagine if you kept accumulating all your draws for 5 years! It would throw your company's equity picture all out of proportion. And, this is true for the Net Income because this number is a carry-over from our previous report, the Profit and Loss or Income Statement. The accounts reported on the P & L statement all get zeroed-out for the start of the new fiscal year, no exceptions. So that makes our Net Income figure start over as well. The Net Income is the "year-to-date" balance after you subtract all your expense accounts from all your income accounts. The figure that appears on your Balance Sheet is for your fiscal year up through the date you are reporting on. For instance, this Balance Sheet is for January through September, therefore this Net Income figure is the year-to-date net profit for nine months of income, less nine months' expenses. It appears on the Balance Sheet for a couple of reasons. For one thing it is very much a part of your company's equity picture. The other thing is, because the Balance Sheet is a report on the cumulative accounts for your company, Net Income fits that criteria as well.

The other equity account—the Retained Earnings—is like the "dump" account for zeroing out these items on the first day of the new fiscal year. Retained Earnings are Profits (or Losses) from earlier accounting periods that are cumulative and remain "in the company," and are not distributed back to the company's owner(s). At the end of your fiscal year your Owner Draw Account is transferred into Retained Earnings. Then the Retained Earnings balance remains the same throughout the year, always reflecting the cumulative total of your previous year's Net Profits. Here's an example:

Say, I've already zeroed-out my Income and Expense accounts, as mentioned previously in the Profit and Loss explanation, and dumped the resulting balance of that into my Retained Earnings account. Now I want to zero-out my Draw Account for my company because I am about to start my new fiscal year and it is my first day. I have drawn a total of $10,000.00 from my company throughout the previous year. (Remember Equity Accounts are Credit Accounts.) My draw account is a Debit balance or negative balance (because I have been "taking from" my company). So I need to ADD to it to make it zero. So, in T Accounts the entries look like this:

Owner Draws
DR I CR
$10,000.00

Retained Earning
DR I CR
$10,000.00

Since my Draw Account had a negative Debit balance I added the Credit amount of $10,000. This will now be removed from my Retained Earnings account which is cumulative of all my previous year's Net Profits and will appear on my Balance Sheet report as the same end result figure every time throughout the upcoming year.

Are you still with me? See how this all fits together like a bunch of puzzle pieces? You know, if you have an easy to use accounting software program on your computer, this would be done for you automatically. If it were an up-to- date program, you wouldn't have to actually make these entries; your computer would do it for you. If you are doing your own books manually, this information is imperative to you. Grasp an understanding of these concepts described here and you can walk with total confidence into any bank, or lawyer, or CPA, or any auditor from any agency because you will be able to believe in the integrity of your own work. Wow! That's freedom! Freedom from any worry around your bookkeeping, or your business, right? Let's move on to the next section.

Chapter Three

THE BASIC BUSINESS STRUCTURES

Small businesses are typically structured in 3 different ways: Sole Proprietorship, Incorporation, [particularly an S-Corp or an LLC], and a Nonprofit Corporation. First, let's look at a Sole Proprietorship:

Sole Proprietorship

In a Sole Proprietorship, you are your business and your business is you. Technically, it doesn't matter if you have a separate checking account, although that helps. All your expenses and income from your personal life and your business life, are one. Likewise, if you are sued, your personal property can be affected. Moreover, if you have a family, this could affect their property too. Along this line, if you are married your spouse could also be responsible for any profits or debts as well. A Sole Proprietorship can be formed anywhere your business is located and can be in place for the lifetime of the individual in whose name it was registered.

If you decide to engage employees, I would suggest getting an Employer Identification Number from the Internal Revenue Service. You can do this by going to the website of irs.gov, download the form SS-4 which can be filled out and then submitted online. It costs nothing and they will email back your new E.I.N. number within the hour. As a Sole Proprietor, you can also use your social security number for all your tax forms, but in this day and age, it is highly unadvisable.

It is likely your state has a state tax I.D. number for businesses. You will want to register your business name with your state and make sure no one else is using that same business name. You can go to your state's Secretary of State website for this which is a good place to start.

You will need the state I.D. number if you are planning to sell any retail items, meaning you will be charging and collecting sales tax. You will also need it if you are providing services, or anything that will bring income to you that will eventually become reportable to your state. You will also need your state's identification number if you are planning to have employees. This will identify you to your state on any state payroll tax forms, such as Unemployment or Workman's Compensation. Later, I will expand on this in the bookkeeping section of the book!

You will need to buy a license to do business within the city or town you live in. Maybe your town has its own website where you can do this, or you can just go to your city's business offices and buy one. This should probably be done after you register with your state and get your state identification number. You may need that information before registering with your city. Some cities and towns are set up so that the individual business licenses are bought when you register and pay for your state's fees. Check with your accounting professional if you are not sure. When checking with the city or town where your place of business is located, consider the fact that you may also be doing business in the surrounding cities or towns and you may also need business licenses for those as well. When visiting your city's offices consider joining your local Chamber of Commerce. Do this especially if you like networking and general 'schmoozing.' It is all good for business!

Should I Take a Paycheck or a draw?

As a Sole Proprietor, you can take 'draws' from your company, which means you write yourself a check out the company. Draws DO NOT affect the net profit of your company. Your net profit is your very bottom line. (There is more about this in the bookkeeping section of this guide.) Another option is to pay yourself as an employee. You can do both if you like. Paychecks DO affect the net profit of your company. As an employee, you will take at least Social Security and Medicare out of your paycheck then your company matches the amounts just as with the rest of your employees. This rate is 7.65% for the employer and the employee for both Social Security and Medicare combined. This is one way to reduce the net profit of your company when tax time arrives. As a Sole Proprietor, you also get to pay a Self-Employment Tax on the net profit at tax time. Self-employment tax is the way the self-employed Sole Proprietor pays into Social Security and Medicare. The current rate for Self-employment tax is 15.3%. The IRS gives a 50% discount on this. So you see, if this is not too confusing, that you will pay the full rate of the combined Social Security and Medicare tax (15.3% for the employer and employee sections), if you take a paycheck. On the other hand, you can pay 50% of the 15.3% Self-employment tax on your net profit. You can also do both. One way or another you will be paying into your Social Security and Medicare.

As you can see, there are choices in regards to taking your pay from your company. As with any new business, you will need to discern which will be the best solution for you. If you decide to become a Sole Proprietorship, you can try different ways and see what works best for you at tax time. One final note, as a Sole Proprietor you are required to file your taxes by April 15th just like all U.S. individuals, because as a Sole Proprietor, your business taxes are your personal taxes.

Incorporation and S-Corp Designation

Incorporation is a possibility for any size company. Some people think you have to be a large company to be incorporated, or a corporation. You do not. You can be incorporated even if you are just one person. I operate my business as an S-Corp. We can look at more on that designation in a moment.

It is not complicated to incorporate. Incorporation is done on a state level so, for instance, in my state of Maryland, I start by going online to the

Marylandtaxes.com. The process is efficient ranging from immediately to a couple days I get a new state identification number for my business and the date of my incorporation confirmed by the state.

Next, if I didn't already have one, I go online to the IRS at www.irs.gov and fill in and submit online a Form SS-4 for a new Employer Identification Number. This is free and they will email the number they have assigned to me probably within the hour.

In a corporation, there are stockholders, a board of directors, and employees. You get to pick who these people are. They can be anybody, even one person— like you! They can be people you know, people interested in investing in your business, family members, anyone. This makes me want to re-emphasize that if you are going into business with other individuals, even family members, you should get a professional such as a lawyer or CPA to help you write up the by-laws of your company. You need a clear and understandable guide as to how the business will affect everyone involved.

That said— there are many advantages to incorporating. One advantage is the officers and stockholders are protected from the debts and liabilities of the corporation. This is because a corporation is a separate legal entity. It has its own life. It can be bought and sold, or passed on to future generations. It could conceivably go on forever. Another advantage is capital can be raised through the sale of stock. Many small corporations have become huge this way.

One big disadvantage to a smaller corporation is that unless an S-Corp status is applied for, incorporating opens the door to double taxation on the profits of your company. This means the corporation is taxed on its profits as income *and* the shareholders are taxed on the profits of the corporation as income to the shareholders. If the corporation plans to remain rather small, an election to become an S-Corp would be desirable and the double taxation would be avoided. An S-Corp does not get its profits taxed as income. The profits (or losses) are passed straight through to the shareholders, therefore the shareholders report the income or loss that is generated by the S-Corp on their individual tax returns. This is proportionate to the percentages held by each officer/shareholder of the corporation. Again, if you are just one person, (like I am in my little S- Corp) you are President, Vice President, Secretary, Treasurer and 'Number One' employee and Stockholder! This also means I am 100% responsible for the profit or loss of my business at tax time.

There are just a few rules to maintain an S- Corp status. First, in order to be considered an S-Corp you have to apply for this status with the IRS. Apply for an S-Corp status *after* you have completed all the other steps for incorporation as directed by the state you are incorporating under. Do this by filling out the IRS Form

2553. (You cannot, as of October 2016, fill this out and submit it online.) You have to download it, print it out, fill it in and mail it to them. I suggest mailing it by certified mail so you have a confirmation of it being received by them on a certain date In order to be considered an S-Corp for the current year, you would have had to submit this form in either the previous year or no later than March 15th of this year. You can send it in any time after March 15th to be considered an S- Corp for the following year.

Here are a few more S-Corp stipulations: the corporation must be a domestic corporation, you can only have one class of stock, no more than 35 stockholders, and the stockholders must be individuals, estates or certain trusts. And, even if your S-Corp is just you, you must pay yourself a "reasonable wage" so you are an employee of your corporation. In addition, you will need to have at least Social Security and Medicare taken out of your check and set aside for taxes. Currently the rate for both is 7.65%. Furthermore, the corporation does match that percentage paid towards payroll taxes to the IRS. The bonus is that you— as the officer of the corporation — can also take a "dividend distribution." This has no payroll taxes taken from it. It is essentially a draw, like in a Sole Proprietorship. It does not affect the bottom line net profits of your corporation. And, you as an individual are not taxed on it at income tax time. There are formulas to help your tax professional decide which portion of your dividend distributions are taxable. You may be responsible for paying a periodic estimated tax on these distributions. For this current information you should definitely contact your CPA.

LLC = Limited Liability Company

So, contrary to popular belief, the initials LLC do not mean Limited Liability Corporation. There is no such legal term. They actually mean Limited Liability *Company*. This business structure has very similar characteristics to an S-Corp so if you read the previous paragraphs on incorporation and the S-Corp, you can get an idea of the LLC structure. The LLC has the limited liability advantages of a corporation. The owners are called 'Members' and the Members are protected from the debts and liabilities of the company. Just like in an S-Corp, you can be a "Single Member" so you can be an LLC all on your own. The LLC enjoys the same freedom from double taxation as the S- Corp does, meaning each Member is responsible for reporting their share of the profit or loss of the company on their individual income tax returns. A difference from the S-Corp is the LLC Member is not required to receive a "reasonable wage" and does not have to be considered an employee. But an

LLC Member is considered to be self-employed and is responsible for paying their own estimated taxes and self-employment tax on the income they do receive from the LLC, however the Member receives it.

Forming an LLC is very similar to forming a corporation. Start your LLC and follow the same guidelines as mentioned in the paragraphs pertaining to incorporation. An LLC has a written operating agreement, or articles of organization, which will specify the time (or qualifying event) for dissolution of the LLC. This is another difference from a corporation. An LLC has a set length decided upon by the organizing Members. When an LLC liquidates, the Articles of Dissolution must be filed with the Secretary of State (and in the state) where the LLC was formed.

Nonprofit Corporation

A Nonprofit Corporation is established for a religious, charitable, educational, artistic, literary or scientific purposes permitted under 501(c)(3) designation of the tax code. Qualifying Nonprofits are granted tax-exempt status by both federal and state authorities.

Articles of Incorporation must be filed with the proper state agency. In Washington, it is the Secretary of State. This document must contain specific paragraphs describing the exact nature of the nonprofit activities.

The nonprofit also must include the adoption of a set of by-laws as part of its formalities. You must apply for tax-exempt status from the state in which you are incorporated as well as the federal government.

For the Nonprofit Corporation to qualify for the 501(c)(3) federal tax exempt status, the IRS Form 1023 must be filled out and submitted within 15 months after the Nonprofit has been officially organized. The federal tax exemption status is effective retroactively to the date when the Articles of Incorporation were filed. Once approved, the company is exempt from payment of federal corporate income taxes and it may receive both public and private grants. In addition, all donations and contributions made to the Nonprofit will be tax deductible of up to 50% of the donor's income.

Some states require the Nonprofit to have a minimum of three directors, some only one, and some can have less than three if the Nonprofit has less than three members. You should check with your Secretary of State's office to find out what the requirements are in your state are. As of this writing, in Washington, only one is necessary. The Nonprofit can have paid employees who have regular payroll taxes taken out of their checks. Then the Nonprofit is responsible for filing the usual periodic payroll taxes that go along with creating paychecks.

Nonprofit Corporations also enjoy the same limited liability protection as profit corporations. Meaning the directors, trustees, officers and/or members are typically not personally liable for the debts and obligations of the Nonprofit. Another similarity the Nonprofit shares with the for-profit corporation is its unlimited life. Once a Nonprofit Corporation is created, like any other corporation, it is its own legal entity that can go on forever.

As always, if there is anything you are uncertain about any of the procedures necessary to get your business structured in the way that is most advantageous for you— by all means— contact your lawyer or CPA for questions or assistance. A little money spent in the beginning of a venture to set it up properly will be good insurance for the duration of your business and will pay off in the end.

(See example of Balance Sheet on next page)

Balance Sheet
As of December 31, 2011 (000s)

Assets		Liabilities	
Cash	481	Accounts Payable	625
Marketable Securities	1,346	Current Portion L-T Debt	1,021
Accounts Receivable	1,677	Taxes Payable	36
Inventory	2,936	Accrued Expenses	157
Prepaid Expenses	172	Total Current Liabilities	1,839
Other Current Assets	58		
Total Current Assets	6,670	Long-term Debt	2,332
		Total Liabilities	**4,171**
Gross Value of Property, Plant & Equipment	2,019	**Stockholders Equity**	
Accumulated Depreciation	(664)	Common Stock and Paid-in Cap	194
Net Property, Plant, Equipment	1,355	Retained Earnings	4,009
		Total Shareholders' Equity	4,203
Note Receivable	349		
Total Assets	**8,374**	**Total Liabilities and Equity**	**8,374**

Chapter Four

PAYROLL BOOKKEEPING

There are many things to know about payroll. First of all, a suggestion to anyone with employees: Make sure you have them fill out a W-4 form. This is the form that has them list their name, address, social security number, and what their deduction status will be on their paycheck. You have probably filled out one of these forms for yourself. It is necessary for your quarterly and year-end reporting. And, if you have had the unfortunate situation of hiring someone only to have them quit after their first paycheck, you will know how hard it may be to track them down for this information if you didn't get it from them at the very start.

Doing your own payroll isn't hard, but payroll taxes do provide a challenge! When you generate a paycheck for yourself, or employees, the Gross Wage ("Gross" is the wage before any taxes are taken out) is recorded as a Debit in your expense account for "Payroll" or "Wages." Or, it can be defined as Gross Wages. The payroll taxes go into the related Payroll Tax Liability accounts as Credits. The Net amount of the paycheck— which is the wage after the taxes come out— is removed from your checkbook also as a Credit entry. Think back to how the Debits and Credits appear when you write a check…let's see how this looks in "T" accounts:

(Expense)
Gross Wages
DR | CR
$500.00

(Current Liability)
Fed. Withholding
DR | CR
$65.00
(Current Liab.)
Soc.Sec. & Med.
DR | CR
$38.25

(Current Liability)
State Disability
DR | CR
$1.50

Checking
DR | CR
$395.25 (Net Pay Check)

See how all the credits add up to the Gross Wage Debit? It seems easy so far. The part that some people find tough about payroll is keeping track of all the taxes. Let me break them down using the above example:

1. Payroll Taxes that are the Employee's
   Responsibility:

#1 Federal Withholding

This also gets abbreviated as FWT, or FIT, (Federal Income Tax). If you are doing your payroll manually, you must have an IRS publication called a "Circular E" and it must be for the current year. Using the W-4 form that I first mentioned in this section, take note of the deduction status the employee provided (i.e. single, married, with 0, 1, or 2, etc. deductions). In the Circular E are pages of tables to help you determine the correct amount of Federal Withholding for the paycheck.

First you choose the pages that correspond to the frequency of your payroll. Do you pay employees weekly (once a week), bi-weekly (every other week), semi-monthly (twice a month), or monthly (once a month)? Then find the section that corresponds to the deduction status as listed on the employee's W-4 form. Then find the Gross Wage of the paycheck, look in the proper column, and find the correct Federal Withholding amount. Federal Withholding is paid entirely by the employee, you are merely deducting it from the paycheck so they can pass it on to the IRS. That is your responsibility as an employer. So, technically you are not withholding your money from the employee's check, you are withholding their money from their check *for them*. This is a very important point to remember as an employer. Let's look at the other taxes then I can tie these different parts together.

#2 Social Security and Medicare

Collectively these add up to 7.65% of the employee's Gross Wage. If we separate them, Social Security is taxed at a rate of 6.2% which has a wage base. That means after an employee's Gross Wage reaches a certain amount in the year from January through December, you don't have to withhold that out of their check for the remainder of that year. Currently the wage base is $84,000. Medicare is taxed at a rate of 1.45% and this has no wage base. In other words, all wages are subject to the 1.45% Medicare. Multiply the Gross Wage by each of these percentages to get the proper deduction amount. (Note: The percentages and wage base mentioned here is current with this writing, consult your

Circular E to make sure of the percentages and wage base at the time you are preparing your payroll, they do change from time to time). And again, you are simply withholding this money from your employee's check for them.

#3 Your State's Disability Insurance

This is a deduction most states have and it is based on the same premise as the federal taxes in that you withhold it from your employee's check <u>for them</u>. In the state of Washington, this is sent to the Department of Labor & Industries. So on the paycheck, it is designated as Labor and Industries, or just L & I. Rates of withholding vary from state to state and sometimes are contingent on the employee's job description, as it is in our state of Maryland. Also in Washington, this is not based on the employee's wage it is based on their hours, therefore you would multiply the employee's rate by their hours to get the proper deduction amount. These are the usual items which are withheld from the employee's paycheck by the employer to be sent in for the employee at the appropriate time. Now we have to look at:

2. Payroll Taxes that are the Employer's Responsibility:

#1 Social Security and Medicare

This is NOT withheld from the employee's paycheck. This is an employer expense. And, once again, check your Circular E publication for the current rate at the time you are reading this. Right now, the employer portion of Social Security and Medicare is exactly the same rate as the employee's as well as the wage base, which is the same too. So, when you make the payment for these items to the IRS for the employee, you make the same payment for the employer. These are totaled together onto the same check along with the Federal Withholding amount you withheld from your employee's paycheck. The frequency of this payment depends on the size of your payroll. If the Federal Withholding, (along with the Employee and

Employer portions of both Social Security and Medicare) are more than $500 in a quarter (Jan.-Mar., Apr.-June, July-Sept., Oct.-Dec.), then you should be making this deposit once a month on the 15th at your bank. Check with your bank to make sure they are capable of receiving payroll tax payments for the IRS. Most do, some don't. When you do pay this check at your bank it will require a "Federal Tax Deposit coupon." This is a small white and blue coupon that goes with your check stating your company name, employer ID number, and amount you are paying. You also must mark in the little oval that corresponds with the proper quarter you are paying for, and the oval marked "941." Or, if your payroll is really big, you may be required by the IRS to pay this on each payroll. If that is the case, they will let you know most likely after your first year. Furthermore, any new companies applying for employer ID numbers are now being asked to pay these taxes electronically either by phone or via the Internet. This is easy with the instructions they send along to you. If in a quarter these combined taxes are less than $500 then you can pay it quarterly without incurring a penalty for lateness. This is done by reporting your payroll amount and total amounts of

Federal Withholding, Social Security and Medicare on the IRS Form 941. It is pretty easy to fill this out yourself each quarter if you have been keeping good records of your payroll.

#2 Federal Unemployment Tax

Otherwise known as FUTA, this is a Federal Unemployment Tax and is generated to cover employees who have lost their jobs. Now, almost every employer has to pay this percentage based on their employee's Gross Wages. Again, all the really detailed information on this tax is in the Circular E. Check it for current rates and how this tax applies to your employment situation. Generally speaking this tax mirrors your state's unemployment tax, so if you are required to pay unemployment tax in your state, then you are also required to follow up with the FUTA.

The current rate as of this writing for FUTA is 6.2%. Most employers are eligible for a credit on this tax of 5.4% so that leaves the total rate of FUTA at .8%. The wage base for FUTA as of this writing is

$7,000., therefore after an employee incurs $7,000 in Gross Wages in a year, somewhere between January through December, you don't have to pay this tax any longer for that employee for the remainder of that year. Again, this is an <u>employer expense,</u> and NOT withheld from the employee's paycheck. FUTA is reported on the IRS Form 940, which is only filed annually after December. However, if your accumulated FUTA gets to be more than $100 in any quarter, you must make a check and pay it through your bank, online or over the telephone in exactly the same fashion as you pay your Federal Withholding, Social Security and Medicare. Meaning you will want to use the Federal Tax Deposit coupons with your check when you take it to your bank. Mark the proper oval for the proper quarter and mark the oval for "940". Make sure FUTA taxes are paid with a separate check.

#3 State Unemployment

Again, this is an employer expense and is NOT withheld from the employee's check. Every state is probably going to be different on this one. In our state of Washington, the rate is based on the employee's gross wage and has a pretty low wage base. But, the percentage rate varies from employer to employer. They base their rates on how many claims you get against your unemployment account. This is paid on a quarterly basis using a form that gets filled out to report your total payroll, less any payroll amounts that are exempt due to the wage base, then multiplying what is left by the employer's rate and that's what is owed for that quarter. Please check with your state's department for unemployment for information on how you are to report for your payroll.

#4 Your State's Disability Insurance

Some states, like our state of Washington, also has an employer portion that gets paid along with the employee's portion. The Department of Labor and Industries designates a rate for a certain type of job, say .50¢cents per hour, and that rate is divided between the employee (.10 ¢ per hour) and the employer (.40 ¢ per hour). This is paid at quarterly intervals on a form that reports your total Gross Wages, and the total hours worked which are multiplied by the one rate (employer and employee rates added together). Please check with your state's department for state disability for information on how you are to report for your payroll.

Yikes! Does this mean you have to set up 7 or 8 different payroll tax liability accounts just to keep track of all this? Well, employees are expensive and complicated, there's no doubt about that! However, 'no' is the answer and I'll tell you how I like to do this. I set up a main General Ledger account in the current liabilities called "Payroll Tax." Under that, I have 4 sub-accounts: Form 941, Form 940, State Unemployment and State Disability. In the Form 941 account, I enter all the employee and employer portions for Social Security and Medicare, and the Federal Withholding. In the Form 940 account, I enter all the FUTA. The State Unemployment account is self-explanatory and then I enter both the employee and employer portions into the State Disability account. That's easy enough, however the real key to all of this— and this is imperative especially if you are doing your payroll manually—

is every time you do paychecks for your employees you must make the entries for your Employer portions of payroll tax as well. (If you are using a handy accounting software program, these entries should be made for you as you generate each payroll check.) So based on the example that was way back at the beginning of this section, let's see how this looks in "T" accounts:

(Current Liability)
FUTA
DR I CR
$4.00

(Current Liability)
State Disability
DR I CR
$6.00

(Current Liability)
State Unemployment
DR I CR
$7.50

(Current Liability)
Social Security/ Medicare
DR ǀ CR
$38.25

(Expense)
Employer's Payroll Tax
DR ǀ CR
$55.75

So, now you can see that $55.75 is the cost to you as the employer to generate a $500.00 paycheck. Of course, this is speculation; your actual numbers may be different. However, please note that this is the portion that gets logged into your Payroll Tax Expense account as the Debit to balance against all the Credits that are going to be included in your Payroll Tax Liability accounts. The employer portion of these payroll taxes is an expense. The credit side to each of these transactions— the portions going to the liability accounts— are being "held" in those liability accounts until they come due for payment. Remember, a portion of the amounts, which are being held in the liability accounts, is actually your employee's tax money, which you are holding for them until it is time to turn it in. Therefore, always please make sure you have enough cash in your checking account to cover the total of your Payroll Tax Liability accounts. It is your responsibility as an employer to be able to send this money in when it is due. And believe me, these government agencies are quick on the draw and you will save yourself plenty in penalties and interest if you can pay these on time and in full!

The last form needed by you as an employer for your employees is the W-2 form. This is the form that everyone is hot for right after December 31st so they can send in their tax return and get their refunds! Actually, I try to convince employees that it is better to 'break even' at the end of the year, that way they get to use their money as they earn it, not giving a free loan to the IRS so they can use the money all year then send a portion of it back. However, for some employees, it is a benefit because it is the only way they can manage to put money aside, which seems like a common issue.

For each employee that you have throughout the year, you must fill out a W-2 form. Even if that employee just took one paycheck you must do a W-2 for each person that was in your employ during the year—January through December— no matter how long or short their employment was, or if they still work for you or not. The W-2 report goes to the Social Security Administration and encompasses the totals for the whole year for each employee's wages; Federal Withholding, Social Security, and Medicare. State withholdings are <u>not</u> reported on this form, however some employee benefits are, such as certain types of medical plans and certain employee perks. If you offer any of these to your employees, check with your CPA to make sure this gets reported correctly the first time around. Believe me, redoing W-2's after the fact is a real pain! You would be glad you did it right the first time! So, let's recap the payroll taxes in an easy to reference list:

Federal Taxes:
Federal Withholding:
Reported on Form 941 quarterly.
Paid monthly (15th), quarterly, or per payroll depending on amount.
Employee paid.

Social Security & Medicare:

Reported on Form 941 quarterly.

Paid monthly (15th), quarterly, or per payroll depending on amount.

Employee and employer portions.

Federal Unemployment tax:

Reported on Form 940 annually.

Paid quarterly or annually depending on amount.

Employer paid only.

Don't forget to check with your state agencies regarding the frequency and forms for your state payroll taxes. These will usually be unemployment and disability insurances. This is the best information I can give you regarding your payroll responsibilities as an employer. If you get really confused regarding rates, reporting times, filling out the forms, etc., please don't hesitate to call the related government agency or look up their website. This is where I had received a lot of my information when I was first starting out. They are always helpful and always willing to set you straight on your information…and most of them are friendly too!

Chapter Five

INVENTORY BOOKKEEPING

If you have a business that has inventory on hand (parts, shop items for sale, etc.), then keeping inventory is a really good tool. What this means is taking an accurate count of your stocked goods on a regular basis. Some businesses like to do it monthly, quarterly, or even yearly. A restaurant I work with likes to do it weekly as it obviously helps them with ordering and planning. Also, they can keep track of wine bottles walking out the door with late night employees! It happens! So whatever your needs are, whatever your business, there is a type of inventory system for you...and your business will dictate how often it is necessary to keep track of inventory items.

To give you an idea, here are some examples of businesses that have a stocked inventory: restaurants, retail stores, job shops [such as auto repair, marine repairs or manufacturing], any business that buys inventory up front to be resold, or used in assembling a product to be sold. If you are a contractor of some sort and only buy parts or materials for use on individual jobs, this doesn't apply to your business. Your purchases simply get recorded under your "Cost of Goods Sold" expense account. Also, if you sell items taken on "consignment" these items are not recognized as inventory and do not need to be counted. (Note: You may not fall in any of the aforementioned categories and may not need to spend time on this chapter!) One thing **is** for certain; every business with stocked goods <u>does</u> need to take at least an annual inventory count by the end of December.

For instance, have you ever wondered why so many retail stores have giant year-end sales? This is specifically to reduce their inventory. The less inventory they have on hand on December 31st, the better it is for the business's tax picture. Here is the reason for that: The IRS needs a figure at the end of the year for Cost of Goods Sold." The way it is figured for tax purposes is to take the starting inventory [as of Jan. 1st], add all the purchases made throughout the year which add to the inventory, plus any labor costs (the owner excluded), plus any materials or supplies relating to the business. From this sum, we subtract the inventory count on Dec. 31st and the result is the figure used by the IRS as "Cost of Goods Sold" which is then a deduction against the income of the business.

It would look like this: Say you just started your business this year and it's a manufacturing shop...

Beginning inventory Jan. 1st = 0.00
Purchases to add inventory = 2,500.00
Assembly worker wages = 10,500.00
Shop supplies = 1,000.00

Sub-total = 14,000.00

Minus year- end inventory = 1,500.00

Total cost of goods sold for tax purposes= $2,500.

Wow! A deduction of $12,500.00 from your income figure can save you a lot in taxes. Of course, this is an ideal situation, but it gives you an idea of what that may look like.

So after you have decided that yours is a business that *does* keep stocked goods on hand, and those goods are regarded and treated as your business's inventory, how do you make the entries to record your purchases and sales, and your cost versus your marked up price? Well, this can be done a couple of different ways depending on what type of business you have. You need to decide how you are going to keep track of your inventory and what system you'll be using for bookkeeping—(a computer program or manually. Essentially, the correct way to do it accounting-wise, (and what a computer program will do for you automatically if you have it set up that way), is as follows:

Here is how it looks in T-Accounts. (Remember "T Accounts" are graphic pictures you can draw of what your accounting entries look like either as you enter them into a manual system, or to help you follow along with your computer.)

Inventory Asset
DR | CR
$500.00 (your cost)

Checking
DR | CR
(your cost) $500.00

When you make a purchase to add to your inventory the 'debit' side of the entry goes into your "Inventory Asset" account. The 'credit' side is to your checking account if you just simply wrote a check for the items, or to your Accounts Payable if you are recording the purchase and planning to make a payment for it at a later date. The amount you are recording in this transaction is the cost of the items, not what you will be reselling them for. As a point of fact, the only amounts recorded in your Inventory Asset account are your costs. And, to recap our previous information, your Inventory Asset account is called this because it is an Asset account, which is a debit account, and is an account that makes up your total asset picture on your Balance Sheet.

That was the easy part, however when you sell the goods, there are a couple of transactions that need to take place. The first part is when you sell an item; your cost is entered as a 'credit' to your Inventory Asset account and a 'debit' to your Cost of Goods Sold expense account. This is how you get the cost of your inventory out of your 'assets', because they are now sold, and into your 'expenses.' Because once you have sold an item out of your inventory it then ceases to be an asset (hanging around indefinitely in your storage room or shop), and becomes an actual expense, as it goes out the door with your customer.

Inventory Asset
DR I CR
(your cost) $500.00

Cost of Goods Sold
DR I CR
$500.00 (your cost)

The last part of this transaction is recording the sale itself. The sale is recorded in just the usual way with the 'credit' side being recorded to your sales, and the 'debit' side being recorded either as a deposit (to your checking account) or into your Accounts Receivable if you have billed your customer for the goods to be paid at a later date. Please note: At the point of sale is the time to record the marked up price for your items; meaning amount for which you are reselling your items to your customers.

Sales (Income)
DR | CR
$650.00 (marked up price)

Checking
DR | CR
$650.00 (marked up price)

So, you see this can be as detailed and meticulous as you want regarding your inventory. In my wide range of customers, I have seen them all choose different styles of keeping track of inventory. I'll give you some examples: One retail shop I work with takes inventory only once a year at the end of December, and each month we make an adjustment based on the average mark-up of the items for sale to move the inventory sold from the Inventory Asset account to the Cost of Goods Sold expense account. Every time this store purchases inventory for resale we debit the Inventory Asset account. Some items are sold for 25% more than purchased and some are sold for 30% more. We take the sales figures from each month and multiply the two sales categories by their respective percentage rates, which is the amount we move from the Inventory Assets to the Cost of Goods Sold. Then at the end of the year when they do their actual inventory count, if the actual count is different from what is in the Inventory Asset account, then we make an adjustment against the Cost of Goods Sold expense account to match the Inventory Asset account to the actual count that was taken. One reason we do this is because the sales out of this store are all done manually. In other words, the sales are not recorded electronically at the point of sale. So it would not be practical to keep track of the individual items sold on a daily basis, and then make all the individual entries, etc. It would be more time consuming than it is worth. These days there is a lot of "point of sale" software available that would allow each sale to be recorded electronically. This type of software can be good for a retail store and it will keep track of your inventory for you automatically as you sell each item—provided, of course, you entered the items as you purchased them in the first place.

I also work with a coffee company. This is technically a manufacturing company who also handles their inventory based on the true accounting principles as I explained above. This is for a couple reasons: One is we use a good accounting software program that does all these transactions automatically. Another is because it is practical to do so. We are only dealing with one product, coffee beans. They are all purchased for basically the same price and, once roasted, they are all sold for basically the same price. Then, once every quarter, we take an accurate physical inventory count and match up the Inventory Asset account against the actual count, followed by any adjustment against the Cost of Goods Sold expense account.

The restaurant I mentioned at the top of this chapter does their inventory weekly. Of course, they need to because their product moves in and out very quickly on a daily basis. This greatly helps them with their planning and purchasing and keeps their food costs down. For them, we use a spreadsheet that has all the items kept in stock at the time, (some of it is seasonal), with all their current costs listed. They simply put in the current count, multiply out the values using the current costs, and get a total. Because the owners are so involved with the financial goings on of the business, they have used this tool to their benefit which has added to their success directly.

So, there you have it- a few case histories! I hope the information in this chapter allows you to decide if one of these methods is right for you. If you are a business that keeps stocked goods, I think you will notice your cash flow tightening up once you start applying a close and consistent method of inventory tracking.

Bank Reconciliation

So many people in business don't know how to reconcile their checking accounts to their bank statements. It seems like a fundamental skill, and if you are one of these people, you are not alone; trust me. However, it is a very important function if you want to stay on top of your checking account balance. If you are like most small businesses, your checking account is one of your main cash sources. So to save yourself a lot of extra fees, and maybe some bounced checks, reconcile your checking account to your bank statement once a month and you will be glad you did. Whether you use an accounting program on your computer, or you are doing it manually, it all gets done the same way. So here is what to do:

With your bank statement open right next to your check register, start checking off the things that appear both in your bank statement and your check register, including any deposits made, checks written, deposits or deductions made to your account by your bank that you have noted in your check register prior to receiving your statement. (Sometimes your bank will send you little slip of paper advising you to do this. Take advantage of these slips of paper by writing the adjustment into your check register when you receive them.) This is a great way to discover any deposits you made, or checks you wrote, but neglected to put them into your checking account balance. By going through this exercise, you also may discover any errors made by your bank!

After checking off all your deposits and checks, you will then need to choose a date through which you are reconciling your checking account. For most businesses this is simply the last day of the month for which you are reconciling. However, there are some businesses that receive their bank statements with a cut-off date somewhere in the middle of the month. If your business is set up like this with your bank, it is okay to use the same date your bank statement uses for the 'ending date.' (You won't gain anything but extra work for yourself by using the last day of the month in this situation.)

The next step is to make a list of all the checks and deposits that you have made up through the ending date you have chosen that do NOT appear on your bank statement. This is why the ending date is important. The date you choose does not affect anything but how many extra checks and deposits you must list that do not appear on your bank statement. It has been my experience that the more of these you have to list, the more chances there are for mistakes to be made in this area. By using the ending date as noted on your bank statement, you will definitely shorten this list if their cut-off for you is in the middle of the month.

This is where I want to make a couple notes to you…You will be doing yourself a great favor if you enter all checks and deposits into your check register as they are made. Regardless of whether your bank says your checks have cleared or not, you should always count your checks written as being absent from your balance. This way if someone hangs on to a check for a little extra time, it won't come as a shock to you when that check finally does clear your account. (Those of you who operate this way know what I am talking about!)

If you are one of those businesses whose bank has your ending date in the middle of the month, you may want to ask them to change that date to the last day of the month. Do this only if you are struggling with the date they have chosen. A bank will switch your ending date to the one you desire, but to do this, of course, they will charge you. However, it is possible.

So, now that you have checked off all the checks and deposits that appear in your check register and on your bank statement and you have made a listing of all the checks and deposits that do not appear on your bank statement up through the ending date you are working with, here is how it all fits together:

There are two sides to deal with now; the bank's side and your check register's side. On the bank's side, start off with their ending balance as usually shown on the front of your bank statement. Take that list you made of all the checks and deposits that do not appear on your bank statement. To the bank's ending balance add the deposits you have made but did not clear as of your statement date, and subtract all the checks you have listed that have not cleared as of your statement date. Hold onto this figure for a minute. Now on your check register's side start off with the balance showing in your check register that is on the same date as you have chosen for your ending date. To your ending balance add any deposits your bank has made to your account, (such as an interest payment), and subtract any deductions your bank has made to your account, such as bank fees or service charges, provided you have not already included such transactions prior to your ending date. This figure should be exactly the same as the end result that you arrived at for the bank's side of this exercise. If it is, congratulations! You are done. Was that hard? After you do it several months in a row, it will get easier and easier.

Note: If you haven't already entered any interest payments or service charges into your check register prior to discovering them on your bank statement, you will want to put them in your register now. If you enter these into your check register after you have reconciled your account, no matter what date you enter them on, go ahead and put check marks by them because you won't be dealing with them again. The check marks in your register indicate transactions that have already cleared your bank account and will not be showing themselves again.

Now, what happens if the figure you come up with on the bank's side and the figure you get on your check register's side is not exactly the same? Well, this means you have some detective work to do. I have a list of problem solving items that I go through to seek out the discrepancy in the unbalanced check register. Starting with the easiest and most obvious errors first here is the list:

✓ Did you pick the correct ending balance out of the check register? Check the date of the ending balance, if incorrect, use the correct one.

✓ Is the math correct in the check register? Using a good calculator, go back to the last known reconciled balance and start adding and subtracting till you come up to your newly chosen ending balance. (You may want to run a paper "tape" on the calculator.) Maybe it's a math error.

✓ Did you record the correct amount of the check or deposit in your register?

✓ Did you skip over a check or deposit in your register? Maybe it is one that never got listed to your register.

✓ Or, maybe there is a check or deposit that should be on your "transactions NOT cleared" list.

Figure out the difference between the two ending figures from the bank's side and the check register's side. Can you divide it by two? If you can, it is an indication that a check got entered as a deposit or a deposit got entered as a check. (A little math trick!) Go back through your check register and see if something got into the wrong column and correct the entry. If you can't divide the difference by two, go back through the comparison process again.

Matching check for check, deposit for deposit. If you start all over at the beginning and go through this process again you are almost certain to find the error here, if the first 3 steps turned up nothing.

If the error is STILL unsolved and you have tried all these things...this is my favorite! Guess what? It might be an **error made by the bank!** Yes, they do make errors. Some banks make more errors than others! If you are constantly finding errors made by your bank you may want to switch banks. One way to seek out a bank error that isn't obvious, is to check the magnetic encoding on your returned checks. (Note: this only works if your bank returns your cancelled checks to you with your statement.) Look at the cancelled checks returned to you by your bank with your statement. In the bottom right corner on the front of your check is a number that represents what the bank cleared your check for. Check to make certain that the encoded number matches the dollar amount shown on your check. If these two don't match, (and I have run across this situation several times) the bank may have used your correct dollar amount on your statement but when the check ran through their system they picked up the incorrect encoded amount. See? Then your ending balance is actually appearing incorrectly on your statement. At this point you will probably have to make a trip to your bank with the cancelled check in question, and your statement and they will have to adjust their records accordingly. But, for the purpose of finishing the task at hand, take the difference between the amount you wrote your check for and the encoded amount and see if this is the amount you are off.

If you are still having trouble getting your check register and your bank to match, you can always take the whole thing to your bank and ask them for help. Most banks usually have a sympathetic person who helps with things of this nature. However, be warned, it has been my experience that this generally only serves to confuse the situation more. However, on a positive note, I am certain that if you go through the process of the steps listed above, you will have great success in balancing your checking account to your bank statement!

Try it out. I know you will be glad you did.

Chapter Six

CHOOSING BOOKKEEPING SOFTWARE

As there here are literally hundreds of choices out there for accounting software, the choices are so vast, it isn't as easy as it sounds to choose! If you have come to the point where you are comfortable entering your bookkeeping information and you want to be more automated than just using a notebook or columnar pad, then you have to make this choice. I am hesitant to make any solid recommendations here. I've found over the years that people's tastes vary in software as much as in any other area of life. There are several considerations, including what's best for your business. What I can share is my experience with a few of them and what I've used in the past.

I mostly use various forms of *Quickbooks* in many of the small businesses I work with. For me, this is easy to teach to someone and it is also user-friendly for anyone who is new to bookkeeping and accounting. I know someone who uses *Quicken* for her business, and that is one program I would not recommend. *Quicken* is very good to use for your home and household bookkeeping, but it is not designed for business use. Once you try and get any useful reports out of it, for instance, you will see why. So don't mix these two up! *Quickbooks* is for business, *Quicken* is for your household.

These days *Quickbooks* comes in many forms too, so depending on the nature of your business you may find one of the *Quickbooks* formats is going to work for you. They even make point of sale versions now, as well as versions for contractors. These all have variances which make them unique to specific industries, so do your research before making a choice. *Quickbooks* is made by Intuit.

I have worked with good bookkeeping software called *Peachtree*. *Peachtree* was one of the very first bookkeeping software programs ever developed. It first appeared in the early '80s and is a bit more sophisticated than *Quickbooks* as far as reporting goes. It is also is easier to use if you do have some bookkeeping background, or if you are very comfortable with the bookkeeping duties your business will require from you.

Cougar Mountain puts out some good modular software, whereas products like *Quickbooks* and *Peachtree* include everything you would need for any scenario that would come up in a small business. The Cougar Mountain products allow you to purchase whatever modules you need. For instance, you can purchase just a Payroll module, or one for Inventory, or for Point of Sale, for example, and build your bookkeeping software for your needs.

The most sophisticated accounting software I have worked with lately is called *MAS-90* made by Sage. This is also a modular software. It is good if you will be doing a lot of selling online. Not a home based eBay business for instance, but if you manufacture a product and have a warehouse full of inventory. Furthermore, if you will be hiring people to process those orders in a shipping department that needs to be linked to the rest of the office, this might be software worth researching.

And for every company I've just mentioned there are a dozens more programs for each business category. There are many modular software programs, lots of all-inclusive software, really sophisticated programs, really simple programs, so be prepared to research them and ask your business peers what software they use. If you can't settle on one brand over another, hunt down someone who uses it and pick their brain! Go on the internet and read blogs. A couple of good websites for researching this very subject are:

FindAccountingSoftware.com
InternetBasedMoms.com.

Seek out and read product reviews, especially if a software company comes out with a different version frequently. One of the good (and bad things) about bookkeeping software is they are always being updated. This is good, I suppose, but it is sad when you learn a version of your favorite software (that you've grown to love and recommended it to your friends) has gone by the wayside in lieu of the latest version which is more expensive and complicated than the original! And... it's filled with unnecessary graphics now and your three-year-old computer slows way down trying to process it all. Not to mention, when the interfaces you were used to have all changed and the once friendly program now seems strange and unfriendly. Oh yes, this happens! So it is good to find out as much as you can before you lock into one brand of software over another.

Keep in mind you will want to choose one brand that you can stick with over the years. This is because as your company gains financial history (and it is all in the format of one bookkeeping program) it will get harder and harder to switch programs and transfer your company's financial history over to a new program.

So much to think about! Makes me wish we all could still get along with just our pencils, calculators and columnar journals! Sometimes, I feel like those days were a lot easier! So much for high tech.

Cheers!

IN CONCLUSION

Well, we've reached the end of what you need to know to get things off in the right direction and on the right foot. I sincerely hope you have found this easy to read and follow. Remember, if you need help with *anything* at all, go directly to the source and ask questions! You will find most governmental agencies, banks, and other institutions pertinent to your business, very easy to get answers from if you just call and ask. It helps them as well if your business structure and bookkeeping system is set up correctly. You may run into that old thing where 'if you ask 3 different people the same question you will get 3 different answers.' My suggestion to you, and what I have done for myself, is to just keep persevering. And, if you need a helping hand, please get in touch with your local independent bookkeeper. In doing so, you will be making a valuable contact. I wish you many happy and stress free years in your business adventure!

Best,

Philippe & Michael

ABOUT   PL CONSULTING, LLC
Philippe Lerner

Philippe Lerner began PL Consulting, LLC in 2008 and has been on a meteorological rise ever since. Named as one of the fastest growing companies by the Baltimore Business Journal two years in a row, Philippe and his ever-growing team take pride in, not just book keeping, but evaluating businesses, forecasting and planning strategic initiatives.

Their emphasis on customer service has led them to an on-going offer as your 'Go To Partner' and

'CFO For Hire.' Their goal has always been to provide clients with an improved bottom line and ultimately—financial freedom. PL Consulting works with over 95 small business owners in the Mid-Atlantic Area, offering a range of customized financial services to improve their customer's bottom line while helping to grow the business at the same time.

Mr. Lerner graduated from Johns Hopkins University in Baltimore with an MBA, and the Touro College of New York with a BS in Finance. Before beginning PL Consulting, he was the Senior Financial Analyst and Assistant CFO for Sinclair Broadcasting, a company with annual revenues of $2 billion dollars. Philippe is multi-lingual, speaking six languages fluently, and resides with his family in Maryland. PL Consulting is a member of the Better Business Bureau and the Maryland Chamber of Commerce. For more information, please go to: www.plcfo.com.

Michael Hammelburger

Michael Graduated from Loyola University in 2009 with a Master's in Business Administration and joined PL Consulting in 2012 as Director of Business Development. He has helped the company grow tremendously in the 4 years since by focusing heavily on client satisfaction, going the extra mile for his clients, and fine tuning the service PL Consulting provides.

To subscribe to Michael's newsletters go to:
http://www.plcfo.com/weekly_tips.html